I WAS TOLD THERE WOULD BE CAKE AT MY FUNERAL

ALSO BY ANNIE SOPHIE LE

The Absence of You
Bloom Under Moonlight
In All My Salt

I WAS TOLD THERE WOULD BE CAKE AT MY FUNERAL

ANNIE SOPHIE LE

Copyright © 2025 by Annie Sophie Le

All rights reserved.

No part of this book may be reproduced in any form or by any electronic or mechanical means, including information storage and retrieval systems, without written permission from the author, except for the use of brief quotations in a book review.

Edited by Misti Wolanski

Cover designed by Anze Ban Virant of ABV atelier design

Book ISBN: 978-1-7775696-6-2

eBook ISBN: 978-1-7775696-7-9

CONTENTS

Weighted	1
The Heavy Weight of Letting Go of the Dead	2
Unmasked	5
The Emptiness of Fool's Gold Nostalgia	6
The Inheriting of Trauma	8
In Which They Call Me a Bitch for Moving Forward and Leaving the Past Behind	9
The Kaleidoscope of a Daughter's Grief	10
The Intertwining	12
I Carry Her with Me	13
In Which I Drown in the Endless Grief	15
How to Move On with a Grieving Heart	17
Burying the Dead	19
Resting in the Sadness	21
Moving On, Moving Forward	23
The Unweaving	25
How to Drown While Healing	26
The Things I Ask Myself Late at Night	27
Love Without a Home	28
In Which I Forgot How to Swim	29
If I Could Leave Myself, I Would	31
My Homeless Love	32
The Quiet After the Storm	33
I Am a Forgery	34
I Told My Therapist, "There Is Too Much."	36
Quiet Heaviness	37
Dandelion Girl	38
The Night of My Surgery	40
Before the Change	41
The Ignorance of Youth	43
I'm a Failed Documentarian	44
The Last of Us	46
The Shades of Grief	47
The Aftereffects of My Brain Surgeries	48
In Which I Write Another Poem About My Dog	49
My Haunting Ghost	51

In Which I Am a Failed Puzzle Master	52
How to Exorcise a Haunted House	53
I'm Trying, I'm Trying, I'm Trying	55
I am Both Here and Gone	57
Alone with My Ghosts	58
I Know What You're Thinking: "Great. A poem about her dog."	60
In Which My Brain Surgeries Were the Reset Button	62
I Laugh Too Loudly for Being This Feral	63
Half Waif, Half Girl	64
I Don't Remember How to Swim	67
I'm an Amalgamation of Spectre and Girl	68
My Heart	69
Counterfeit Caring	71
In Which I'm too Spiteful To Let My Traitorous Body Win	72
I Can Miss the Past While Still Wanting to Burn Down the Haunted House	73
The Unknowing	74
I Can't Believe It Has Been Sixteen Months	75
Liking My Reflection	76
Good Misfortune	77
One Night	78
Almost Dying Brought Me Here	80
Comedy of Horrors	81
The Irreversible Nature of Life	83
Drown Myself in Softness	84
I'll Survive These Sharp Edges Because I'm Stubborn	86
Sunshine Girl	88
Unencumbered and Untethered	89
There is Grief in Losing	91
I Make Jokes About My Vision Loss to Cope	92
Remembering the Little Moments	94
Despite	95
In Which I Am Given an Award for My Courage and Commended for My Positivity During My Rehabilitation (or) In Which I'm a Contrary Asshole	97
I'm Too Bored to Remain the Same	99
Laughing Too Loudly	100

In the Last Three Years	101
Tiny Little Burdens	103
In Which I've Said "I love you" More Now Than I've Ever Had Before	105
How Completely I've Changed, How Utterly Different I Am	106
I Am Who I Am and Yet I Am Not	108
Moving On, Moving Forward	110
My Stubborn Thriving Heart	112
Great. Yet Another Poem on My Sudden Will to Live and Shining Gratitude	114
On the Days When the Grief Is Too Heavy to Carry	116
I Guess My Two Brain Surgeries Are Blessings in Disguise	118
I Had So Many Plans for Last Year (The Lies I Tell Myself)	119
The Time It Takes	121
The Unfurling	123
My Body—the Bastard—Tried to Kill Me but I Won	125
In Which I've Moved On	128
Coffee and Bitter Truths	130
The Dichotomy of Being Here but Missing	131
Despite the Vision Loss, I Can See Clearer Now Than Before	133
In Which I Cover My Home in Sticky Notes	135
Am I an Asshole?	137
The Cyclical Nature of Being Sad and Being Happy	140
When?	141
Stuck in the Middle	142
2024	144
Growing Pains	146
I'm Too Impatient to Be a Saint	149
Loving Wholly	150
These Days	152
Being Present	154
This Is the First Poem I've Finished in a Year and I'm Going to Celebrate with Ice Cream	156
What I'm Told	158
The Bittersweetness of Life	160
In Which I'm a Sarcastic Asshole, Part I	161
Forgiving Myself for a Lifetime of Self-Immolation	163
How to Survive the Enduring Grief	165

In Which I Decide to Give Living a Try	167
Defiantly Beginning Anew	168
Before and Now	170
Growing a Garden in My Bones	172
How to Get Whiplash by Moving Forward While Missing the Past	173
In Which I'm a Sarcastic Asshole, Part II	175
In the Past Three Years I've	176
How Contrary I've Become	177
In All the Ways, in Every Way	178
In Which I'm Grateful to the Glenrose Hospital for My Rehabilitation but I'm Moving On	180
Comedic Tragedy	182
Lighting Myself on Fire so I Can Float Away	183
The Resiliency of Weeds	184
The Unraveling	186
I'm a Greedy Jerk	188
Acknowledgements and Thanks	191
Ways to connect with me	197

and its name was grief

WEIGHTED

Some days,
the grief is too heavy
to carry.

THE HEAVY WEIGHT OF LETTING GO OF THE DEAD

The sky fell the day I learnt
my mother had cancer.

"Stage four," the doctors said.
"Metastasized throughout her body," they said.
"Only a few days—at most weeks—left," they said.

I saw her sitting on the hospital bed
and broke down in tears.
She opened her arms and hugged me,
all of the years of tumult and anger
between us
gone.

I didn't tell her that day
that her life was on a countdown.
How can you tell your mother she's dying?
How can you explain
you only have a few weeks left with her?
That she wouldn't make it to Mother's Day.
No more birthdays or holidays with her.
How could you break her heart?

She was the one
who brought me into this world,
and now I was the one
to watch her slip from it.
Even though I didn't tell her
any of this that day,
she knew.
She could read the grief on my face,
the truth in my eyes and my trembling hands.

Her strength was insurmountable,
her pain unimaginable,
but she never complained,
never handed me her grief.

Even at the end
she worried about me,
holding me with love.
Even at the very end
she remained strong
and told me not to fuss.

And when she slipped away that night,
when her body finally gave up,
I waited,
thinking it was a nightmare
I'd awaken from.

But neither of us woke up.
Not her from death.
Not me from the nightmare.

It's been years,
and I still forget she's gone,
think both of us are living.
But then I remember she's dead,

gone and in the past.

I'm angry at how unfair it is,
grieving the years she'll never have,
but I try not to hold onto her ghost,
wanting her to rest.

UNMASKED

I sat with my anger for so long
until it whispered its true name.
Grief.

THE EMPTINESS OF FOOL'S GOLD NOSTALGIA

At first I tell myself it doesn't matter
that I was abused by my mother as a child.
I disregard the nights of hunger and angry hands,
the cutting words and pinching fingers.

I tell myself it doesn't matter
because she's dead,
and the past is behind me.
I tell myself I exorcised the ghosts
and have moved on and moved forward.

But then I remember the little girl,
so desperate to be loved,
who became such a twisted and bitter thing.
I remember the cutting anger,
the digging hurt and enduring loneliness.

I remember,
when I remember so little these days,
and can finally speak my truth.

I won't embellish my past with fool's gold
or demonize the memories.

I move forward
and I'm moving on.

There are some days
that are easy and light,
and some days
are heavy and burdened with grief.
I won't saint a woman just because she's dead,
and I won't demonize what is behind me.
The past exists and cannot be changed,
and I'm okay now.

THE INHERITING OF TRAUMA

It's taken me years to realize
my mother did the best she could
with what she knew,
having known abuse as a child
and feeding me from the same plate.
That love was cruel and painful,
and the only way I could be loved
was through hurtful words and angry hands.

After years spent in therapy and treatment,
I excised the threads of learned trauma
and the cycle of abuse from my bones,
which held me together for so long.

In her twisted way,
my mother loved me
the only way she knew how.
And when she died,
I released her ghost
and my childhood hurt.
I gave myself space to heal.
I finally let myself breathe.

IN WHICH THEY CALL ME A BITCH FOR MOVING FORWARD AND LEAVING THE PAST BEHIND

They tell me,
these people who pretend they know me
because of our shared blood,
I should be ashamed for letting years
separate my mother and me.
I should be suffocating under the guilt
for not loving the woman who birthed me,
a woman dead and gone.
They try to fill my pockets with remorse and rocks,
wanting me to drown in an ocean of shame.
But they don't matter to me anymore,
their words slipping over my skin,
skin I no longer wish to cut to shreds.
Our shared blood is meaningless
after years of being their plaything to hurt.
I've grieved for my mother and our past.
I've moved on when they try to hold me back.
I've flown away and left them behind
to rot.

THE KALEIDOSCOPE OF A DAUGHTER'S GRIEF

Years separated my mother and me,
the distance growing into a yawning chasm
between us.
But when I saw her on that hospital bed,
frail and so different from the mother
of my childhood,
I fell apart.

Without hesitation,
she opened her arms and comforted me.
Despite our relationship
having always been tumultuous and hard,
it was suddenly easy to fall back
into a child's love for her mother.

I was told by countless doctors
she had less than a month to live,
her body eaten away from cancer.

I didn't have hope for a future together
but I hoped she wouldn't be in pain
for the time she had left with me.

Despite knowing our time together was finite
and her drowning
in increasingly unbearable pain,
she comforted me.
Despite our hardships with each other,
she still loved me.

And as she brought me
into this world with love,
I stood by her side with love
when she slipped away.

THE INTERTWINING

How deep the love and grief go.

I CARRY HER WITH ME

Some days it's too raw
to carry the memories
of my mother with me.
Too heavy to remember
the roughness shared between us
and the years which separate us.

It's hard to remember the good,
the easy laughter and shared love.
Harder still to remember the painful things,
cruel and sharp and abrasive.

There are days I forget she's gone,
and other days,
all I feel is her absence.
Her death didn't erase
my childhood wounds and hurt.
It didn't soften my rough edges,
but now I no longer cling
to decades of aches.

I can hold onto memories of her,
without the edges cutting my palms.

I can breathe through the grief,
remembering the bitter days,
and the good days.

I release her ghost and know
I'll always carry her with me
wherever I go.

IN WHICH I DROWN IN THE ENDLESS GRIEF

There's this yawning,
gaping hole
which eats
and eats
and eats away at me.
Devouring everything it touches,
eroding my calm
when I think the day
is a going to be good.

It reminds me of my losses
and how different everything is now.
Nothing is the same
and will never be again.

Aching and hurting and stinging,
little reminders of mourning,
bitter paper cuts of grief.
All consuming,
rendering me breathless
from the bottomless hurt,
poking and prodding and demanding
I pay attention to these phantasms

always trailing me.

When will I be released
from their grasp?
When will I be able to breathe
through the endless grief?

HOW TO MOVE ON WITH A GRIEVING HEART

I could never understand
why my mother hurt me the ways she did.
Letting me feast on curdled milk from her tit,
sewing years of trauma into my skin.
The tears I spilt as a child
only fuelled her frenzied anger.

In my spiteful teenaged years,
I turned the rage inwards,
trying to cut myself to pieces,
hoping I could quiet the phantoms.

During those years,
I questioned my worth,
wondering why I was so hard to love
that not even my mother could love
such a hollow and gnarled girl.

In all the years since,
I never found the answers.
As my mother lay dying,
I realized I no longer cared to ask her
why she had hurt me,

and why was I so hard to love?

Because even if I had the answers,
I realised I didn't care enough to hear them.
They no longer held power over me,
and I wouldn't hold onto the hurt.
I had moved on and outgrown
my teenage rage.

And when she died,
I allowed myself the freedom
to grieve for the absent girl I was
and the years lost between us.
I mourned what we could have been.

I grieved and finally let myself
move on.

BURYING THE DEAD

Even though years had separated
my mother and me,
I don't feel guilt or shame.
I know now I had to excise
the hurt from my bones,
give myself time to heal.

For my mental health,
I had to drain my endless anger,
tell myself hurt doesn't heal
in the span of a night.
Remind myself that guilt
is just another way to hurt myself
and I'm tired of suffocating
under years of shame.
Shame which was never mine to carry.

I remember the good days between us,
and the days of being hurt
by her cruel hands and vicious words.
I've grieved for the little girl I used to be,
a waif so desperate to be loved,
and the twisted and bitter woman she grew into.

I've grieved for my mother
and the lost years between us,
but I won't dig up the dead anymore.

I'm letting the past rest,
moving forward
and giving myself space to breathe.

I can feel the sunshine on my face,
after years of shrouding myself
in wounds and darkness.

RESTING IN THE SADNESS

I try to remember the love between us
in the memories I remember,
when I'm able to remember at all.
I try to live fully to honour the gone
and live for the both of us.
I try and try and try.

Some days I come alive,
completely and gratefully.
I want to live and cherish
the love we once shared.

And then there are days
when the sadness is too much,
when the ghosts cling to me,
unwilling to let go.

I don't know which day
will unfold when I wake up.
Will I float in a sea of laughter
and lightness?
Or will I slip into the cacophony
of grief and regret?

I'll allow myself to rest on the days
when the clouds are too heavy.
And I'll flourish on the days
when I can feel the sunshine
on my tender skin.

Today the memories are weighted,
but I won't cling to the darkness like I used to.
I won't sew brokenness into my flesh,
or make a home in the shadows.

I'll allow myself to rest in the heaviness
and tomorrow I'll try again,
hoping to feel the sun
once more.

MOVING ON, MOVING FORWARD

Thanks to years of therapy,
I realized my mother
wasn't only darkness,
and my father wasn't a saint.

Both were human,
incomplete with flaws
and imperfections.
I stopped vilifying
my mother's memory
and glorifying my father
in his old age.

I don't hold anger
against either of them anymore,
even if moving on
is heavy some days.

I'm not making excuses
for my mother's abuse,
for my father's absence,
but I realized they were
flawed,

young,
and stupid.

I'm not going
to encase myself in bitterness,
or force myself to live in the past.
I've learned to let go,
and by letting go,
my darkness has let go of me.

And in the space between
letting go and holding on,
I've found myself.
And I will learn to live.

THE UNWEAVING

I've scraped
my ribcage bare,
trying to find
where the grief ends
and I begin.

HOW TO DROWN WHILE HEALING

My therapist told me one day
when I broke down in tears,

> *"Annie, grief isn't a one-way street.*
> *It's not something you get over.*
> *It's a cycle of constancy*
> *and a ghost following you*
> *wherever you go."*

And I told her through tissues and tears,
feeling broken and raw and hurt,

> *"Grief and healing are assholes.*
> *For the first time in my life,*
> *I'm finally coming alive,*
> *only to pulled back under the weight*
> *of all of this loss."*

THE THINGS I ASK MYSELF LATE AT NIGHT

Lately I've been falling apart
at unexpected moments
and in the oddest of times.

When I'm washing my hair.
When I'm cooking dinner.
When I'm pouring myself a glass of water.

The sadness is perpetual and enduring,
never leaving,
always there.
Waiting,
lurking,
weighing me down.
Down, down, down.

If I'm not grieving for what I've lost,
will I forget it all?
If there is no grief,
was there ever love?

LOVE WITHOUT A HOME

I'm told
the grief will always be there,
following me wherever I go,
but will look different
and come in waves.

I'm told
I'll never be able to get over the grief,
and it will always be in my life,
but I'll learn to live with it.
It's my shadow,
a constant companion
I wish I could exorcise.

I'm told
grief is just another word
for love without
a home.

IN WHICH I FORGOT HOW TO SWIM

I broke down last night,
cried for all I've lost.
Lost hopes and opportunities,
lost chances and possibilities,
lost love and lost me.

Though I like myself more
than I ever have before,
and for the first time in my life,
I don't want to disappear
or tear myself to shreds,
I grieve.

And despite being able to feel
the sun on my skin
for the first time in my life,
the ache is unforgiving and persists.

I know the grief
won't always be as crushing
and one day I'll be able to breathe
through it.

But today I'll let myself sink
beneath the tidal waves
of sadness.
Today I'll let myself
drown.

IF I COULD LEAVE MYSELF, I WOULD

People are tired of my grief
always trailing behind me.
They are annoyed by my laughter
when it's suddenly torn apart by the sadness,
always lurking in our peripherals.
They look away when my smiles grow brittle,
and disregard my needing outstretched arms.
I don't blame them for leaving me,
when I would leave myself too.

MY HOMELESS LOVE

I always thought grief was a one-way road,
landmarks to pass and move on from.
But grief isn't linear,
not something to feel and release,
never to be felt again.
Grief is unending and constant.
Some days it's soft and nostalgic,
and other days it's biting and cruel.
I try to remind myself
I feel grief
because I've lived and loved and lost.
I grieve
because my love has nowhere to go.

THE QUIET AFTER THE STORM

I want to feel calm,
to be at peace
with these changes
and who I am now.
Maybe one day soon,
the grief will lessen
and won't be as heavy.
Maybe soon,
I'll be able to breathe again.

I AM A FORGERY

My laughter and smiles
put others at ease.
*(Do they mirror those around me
or are they genuine and true?)*

Because nothing makes people
more uncomfortable than crying.
Because sadness emphasizes
the space between us.
Because no one wants to admit
how irrevocably I've changed.
(I'm just a forgery of my old self)

I hide behind smiles and laughter
and hold back
the sadness,
the tears,
the grief.
*(I guess it's true what they say
about jokes cloaking the truth)*

I'm nostalgic
for the worst times in my life

because they're familiar.
(Even if the familiar hurts)

So here I am today,
storm clouds trailing behind me,
and I struggle beneath the sadness
weighing me down.
*(I can't seem to reconcile
who I was and who I am now)*

Even though it hurts,
all pinpricks and cutting emptiness,
I allow myself to sink into the familiarity
of the grief and hurt and sadness.
*(Hello again,
bitter assholes)*

Today,
I let myself drown
and hope tomorrow
I'll pull my jagged pieces
back together
and feel the sunshine
once again.
*(I'll use nails and tape and glue
if I have to)*

I TOLD MY THERAPIST, "THERE IS TOO MUCH."

Too much grief.
Too much loss.
Too many stinging edges
which dig and burn and cut.

But she told me,

> "Annie,
> there is still light in the shadows.
> Happiness can coexist alongside the grief.
> You can be undone by gratitude
> but still ache with loss.
> You've made it through hell,
> yet stumble under the heartbreak.
> You will survive these edges too."

QUIET HEAVINESS

And it is here in the quiet moments
when I'm alone
that the memories come to me.

The phantoms lurk,
always lurking,
seeping under my skin,
slipping into my veins,
finding a home in my marrow.

I remind myself I'm strong
but it's in the quietness that I break.
I give myself over
to the lurking sadness,
drowning in an ocean of tears
and bitter regrets.

I let myself be in the grief
because tomorrow,
I'll try again.

DANDELION GIRL

Flowers grow from decay in the soil,
and even weeds are able to grow
between the cracks in the concrete.
So maybe one day,
I'll be able to breathe through the loss.
And maybe one day,
I'll learn to thrive in both
the drowning and the unfurling,
hoping I'll make it through this
and flourish.

The Excising of Me

THE NIGHT OF MY SURGERY

I fell asleep as
Annie,
the feral child.

And woke up as
Annie,
the lost girl.

BEFORE THE CHANGE

As I left my home with paramedics,
about to be transported to the hospital,
my dad said,

"I'll see you soon."

And life as we both knew it
was forever changed.
We were changed.

Now that we've tasted
the abruptness and fragility of life,
it's hard to look around
and see all the loss.
I look at my loved ones
and wish I could bury them in my heart
so they are always with me
wherever I go.

I am vigilant,
always vigilant,
against loss,
against illness,

against darkness,
worried what will become of us
in the days not yet born.

My obsession with grief,
the constant tumult of sadness and anger,
will I ever let go of them?
Or will they stay with me
and I'll learn to live
with their bitter and cutting edges?

THE IGNORANCE OF YOUTH

In our youth,
we're arrogant,
thinking we're invincible.
We think nothing can touch us
and we have long lives ahead of us.
But our lives and all we have
are not promised to us.
I've lost so much these past few years.
I wonder how much more heartbreak
I can carry with me
before I shatter into a thousand shards
for someone else to carry.

I'M A FAILED DOCUMENTARIAN

I regret not taking more photographs
of my life before the surgeries.
When I felt safe in my life,
in this little bubble
of thinking I'm untouchable.

I go through photo after photo
of everything I left behind and those I lost,
filled with aching grief and bittersweet nostalgia.
Reminders I was lucky
to have had reasons to not slip away,
to have known a life before the one I have now.
I should be grateful to be alive,
beyond thankful to have experienced
a lifetime before this one.

When I look in the mirror,
I compare who I was against who I am now.
I weigh my bones and judge
if I'm just as worthy.
Do I like myself more now,
or do I miss my ghost?

I regret not documenting
my life from before
because my memory is failing these days,
and I wish I could flip through
the reminders of a life I once had.
Though now they're heavy
with bitter nostalgia.

I have to relearn to live
and spend the rest of my life
hoping I won't forget
what I left behind.

THE LAST OF US

The last time I saw my dog,
my dad was holding her back
as I left with the paramedics for the hospital.
I didn't know it then,
when I kissed her goodbye,
it would be the last.

The last kiss,
the last hug,
the last of her,
the last of us,
the last of all I knew.

Fourteen years together,
fourteen years of not feeling alone
because she was with me
through the darkest days of my madness.

Now I have a lifetime without her,
a lifetime of fading memories
of us.

THE SHADES OF GRIEF

Some moments,
I don't think I can go on,
despite surviving so much.
But I do.

Despite what I've lost,
despite the suffocating
weight of grief,

I breathe.
I live.
The ache is still there,
but so is the love.

THE AFTEREFFECTS OF MY BRAIN SURGERIES

and it's like this that I lost all I knew
and it's like this that I lost myself

IN WHICH I WRITE ANOTHER POEM ABOUT MY DOG

I still expect to see her
when I come home.
I still wake up and reach for her,
wanting to feel her soft fur
beneath my fingers
when the hopelessness
becomes crushing.

I wish I could end this poem
by promising myself
I'll see her once again when I'm gone,
but I don't believe in much these days,
and I don't believe in an afterlife.
The dead stay dead,
and the living are forced
to continue without them.

So I'll move forward,
wishing there were days
I could go back.
I'll live,
with some days brighter

than the bitter grief haunting me.
So that's it.

MY HAUNTING GHOST

These days I forget
what I'm doing,
if I've eaten,
what I just said.

I don't know what is real,
or if I've conjured it
from the air.

Desperately trying to find
humour in the darkness.
Lying to myself daily,
that I'm okay,
still whole and unscathed.

If only I could lose myself
in the laughter,
regardless if it's empty or sincere,
reality wouldn't be as crushing,
and I wouldn't feel
half-here and half-gone.

IN WHICH I AM A FAILED PUZZLE MASTER

I'm a jigsaw puzzle
with missing pieces,
so many lost,
I wonder
how I'll ever put myself
back together
and be whole again.

HOW TO EXORCISE A HAUNTED HOUSE

I mourn for who I was,
my forgotten memories
and those I left behind.

I cry over spilt milk
and my lost vision.

I try to console myself
when it all becomes too much.

Tell myself I'm alive and haven't lost
all of my vision,
all of my memories,
all of who I am.

If I tell myself this,
regardless of its bittersweet edges,
will I be able to breathe again,
past the aching hurt?

Will I be able to move forward
without holding onto the ghosts?

Will the ghosts who try so desperately
to hold me back
finally release me?

I'M TRYING, I'M TRYING, I'M TRYING

What started as a migraine
led to two brain surgeries,
saving my life.

But left me with
a waning memory,
vision loss,
cognitive impairments,
epilepsy,
and nerve damage.

In my last memories of that night,
I said goodbye to my dad,
kissed my dog,
left for the ER in an ambulance,
sat on a hospital bed,
spent hours receiving intravenous medication,
and followed the nurse for a CT scan.

Then I woke up.

With a dead dog,
and a patchwork skull

in a new body.
A different person.

No longer feeling safe in my body.
No longer seeing like I used to.
No longer who I was before.

So here I am.
Alive and trying.

Trying to live.
Trying to make this body a home.
Trying to be Annie,
whoever the hell that is.

And even though I spent
a lifetime wishing to disappear
and vanish into the air,
wishing I would no longer be,
I'm relieved and learning to thrive.

Alive
and utterly grateful
I'm here.

I AM BOTH HERE AND GONE

I feel like I'm missing
from my own life.

ALONE WITH MY GHOSTS

My dog and I
were together for fourteen years.

She was with me on my best days
and on the days when I hated
the beating of my heart.

She was there when I tried
to find worthiness in starvation
and answers in my bones.

She was there
when I ripped myself to shreds,
wanting to vanish into the air.

She was all I had throughout the years
when I couldn't see through
my melancholic madness.

She was my everything
when not even my body felt like home.

She was the reason for moving forward
when I thought I had nothing left of me.

She was the beating of my heart
when I wished it would stop.

We were together for so long.
Now I have to relearn to live without her,
on my own
with only my ghosts.

I KNOW WHAT YOU'RE THINKING: "GREAT. A POEM ABOUT HER DOG."

I.
I spent fourteen years with her by my side.
She was both my shadow and my lighthouse,
a buoy keeping me afloat
in a self-destructive tidal wave.

She was my reason for living for so many years,
a salve to my hurting soul,
a bandage around my raw heart.

She was the reason I
never gave in,
never gave up,
never let myself slip under.

II.
There are moments when I look around
expecting to see her,
reaching out to touch her fur,
only to touch air instead.

But then I remember
the brain surgeries,

the month in the ICU,
the days lost to my illness.
All without her.

The last moment I had with her,
before the paramedics took me to the hospital,
was kissing her head
as she stared up at me so innocently,
so hopeful I'd be back.

III.
But when I returned home,
she wasn't there.
I have nothing left of her,
but my failing memories.

I was changed,
my life changed,
everything changed.

I still can't think of her
without shattering into tears.
I can't breathe through the heaviness
when I look around expecting to see her.

IV.
I'm trying to live fully
to honour her memory.
When the grief is too cutting
and I can't breathe past the hurt,
I try to remember the lightness I felt
when she was with me,
and the days spent together,
when she was my reason to stay.
Now I have a lifetime without her,
a lifetime of being my own reason.

IN WHICH MY BRAIN SURGERIES WERE THE RESET BUTTON

The surgeries were a reset
to start over and live my new life.
Sometimes I struggle with who I am now,
wishing I could be angry
at the unfairness of life
and maybe I will be one day.
But for now,
I'm trying to survive the days,
getting to know myself wholly,
craggy edges and softness and all.
I'm learning to accept
my new life,
this new me,
my new everything,
and find grace to give myself time.
Allow myself to feel grief on some days,
let myself laugh on the brighter days,
and rest on the days in-between.

I LAUGH TOO LOUDLY FOR BEING THIS FERAL

I am utterly grateful to be alive
(who would've thought the feral
self-destructive girl
wants to live?)

Though my smiles
are sincere these days
and laughter spills easier now,
the burdensome sadness
still lines my pockets,
heavy from others handing me
their grief.

Being alive is bittersweet and cutting,
and though it hurts,
I'm trying to hold on
to whatever memories remain,
looking for the beauty between
the cracks of loss and mourning.

HALF WAIF, HALF GIRL

One of my doctors told me
during my weekly check-up appointments,
that I won't return to who I was before
and won't get *"better"*—
whatever *"better"* means.

It's only a matter of my brain
remaining stable or declining.
The nerve damage and trembling in my limbs,
the memory loss and vision impairment
are permanent.

My fear of no longer being me
was all encompassing,
all consuming.
To hear it said so plainly,
so bluntly,
was devastating.

A lifetime of waning memories.
A lifetime of guaranteed differentness.
In this endless cycle of mourning,
I'm reminded daily of all I've lost.

Lost pieces of my memories.
Lost pieces of my cognition.
Lost pieces of my vision.
Lost pieces of myself.

There are moments
when I like this new me.
I can finally breathe
and feel comfortable in my my new body,
but these moments are burdened
with hidden heartache,
always there,
waiting beneath my skin.

I'm grateful I'm alive.
The once self-destructive girl
now thirsty for life,
but the cost was steep.

Sometimes I wonder
if it was worth surviving
or if would it have been easier
to slip away.

So that's it.

This is me.
This is who I'll be now.
I know I'm more than my disorders,
I know this.
I know, I know, I know.

But sometimes the whisperings of the phantoms
are deafening in the silence,
louder than the laughter.
I can't help but worry I'll be treated differently,

obscured by my disorders.
Half-human and half-waif.

I try not to fixate or let all of this
gnash on my bones
until nothing is left of me.

I wish this poem had a cheerful ending,
filled with hope and bursting
with excitement.
But it doesn't.

Today this poem ends bitterly,
rough and abrasive,
sorrowful and melancholic.

So I'll sink under the waves of grief
and simply be,
letting myself float away
from here.

I DON'T REMEMBER HOW TO SWIM

I thought
foolishly and naively
that recovery would return me
back to the Annie I was
before the brain surgeries.
I held onto this empty hope,
so bitter and cruel,
that the grief would ease
and I'd be able to breathe again
without drowning.
But the loss persists,
gnawing and digging and tearing
and I'm suffocating
beneath the heaviness.
I wish I could remember
how to swim.

I'M AN AMALGAMATION OF SPECTRE AND GIRL

One moment I'm here
and the next,
I'm gone.
Missing
from me.
Missing
from my own life.
Missing
and yet,
newly birthed,
wholly changed,
irrevocably different.
I'm here but lost,
transformed but still the same.
I'm Annie but I'm not,
and through all of this tumult,
I remain.
Lost girl now found girl.

MY HEART

The grief was heavy last night,
and as I brushed my teeth I cried
when I realized
this is it for me.

I won't return to before.
Before the brain surgeries.
Before the disorders.
Before I lost all I knew.
Before I became half-girl and half-ghost.
Before, before, before.

I like myself now.
I don't want to disappear,
and I don't want to tear
myself to shreds.

And yet the grief remains,
the ache still abrasive.
The ghosts are unrelenting
in haunting me.

If only I could exorcise
the grief from my body.
If only I could excise my heart,
I'd be free of the ache in my chest.

COUNTERFEIT CARING

Since waking up
from the haze of my brain surgeries,
I'm treated differently.
Some without malice.
Others with quiet cruelty.

And suddenly,
I have no independence or personhood.
I'm no longer deserving
of humanity or dignity.

I'm just a rag doll to drag around
and have her limbs
twisted and distorted
by those who say
they care.

IN WHICH I'M TOO SPITEFUL TO LET MY TRAITOROUS BODY WIN

They say I'm upbeat and positive,
that I can still laugh
despite my unsteady health
and many hospital visits.

But I want to tell them,
every damn time,
what other choice do I have,
except to be grateful I'm alive,
despite my treasonous body?

What do I have left to give,
other than my easy smiles
and easier laughter?

They tell me I should be thankful
for their so-called kind words.
But how can I not be offended
when they praise me
for just trying to survive?

I CAN MISS THE PAST WHILE STILL WANTING TO BURN DOWN THE HAUNTED HOUSE

Doctors commend me for being upbeat.
Rehabilitation therapists appreciate how positive I am.
Everyone mistakes my jokes and smiles for happiness,
assuming this new me is who I've always been,
and maybe this is who I'll be now.
But how much deeper will I have to dig
until the venomous girl I used to be is unearthed,
reborn stronger and more vitriolic,
on fire and ready to burn those who come too close?
How much further until I'm me again?
How much longer must I wait
until I can dive back into my ocean of salt
and let the riptides pull me under?
And my scariest fear is,
do I even want to return to that?
Do I want to be that lost girl again?

THE UNKNOWING

My grief comes in waves.
One moment I'm here,
and the next I'm back.

Back to when I was still me.
Back to when I knew who I was.
Back to when my dog was still alive.
Back back back.

Some days,
I give my grief
space to unfurl and exist.
And other days,
I breathe past
the memories and pain and hurt.

I move forward,
unsure of who I am
but no longer holding on
to what is behind me.

I CAN'T BELIEVE IT HAS BEEN SIXTEEN MONTHS

since my dog died
since I left in an ambulance as the venomous girl
since I woke up irreversibly changed as the sunshine girl
since I lost bits and pieces of myself
since I lost complete independence and autonomy
since everything changed.

It has been sixteen months,
and I still feel like I'm missing
in this new body and new life.

But I'm trying.
Trying to make a home in myself.
For once,
trying to embrace being alive.

LIKING MY REFLECTION

There are days which taste bitter,
when rainclouds follow me around,
and I wonder if the cost of surviving
was too steep to pay,
leaving me half a girl.
Here but gone.

The grief is heavy,
too heavy to carry.
I miss what I left behind.
I miss my vision and memories.
I miss who I was.
I miss who I thought I'd become.

I try to lighten the melancholic heartbreak
by reassuring myself
I'll see the sun again,
past the rainclouds
and through the thunderstorms.

I'll be able to see myself.

GOOD MISFORTUNE

I joke about how different I am,
laughing at my failing vision
and memory loss.

I joke about almost dying,
laughing at my good misfortune.

Laughing is easier
than the heavy silence of grief.
It's easier than drowning
in the heaviness of what I lost.

ONE NIGHT

And everything I knew changed,
all that I was—
gone.
Forever different.

The blissful ignorance
of thinking my body was a safe haven,
the arrogance of thinking
I was untouchable by death,
was ripped away.

I'm grateful to be alive,
but this gratefulness
is tempered with unyielding sadness
and acerbic anger.
Over all of these changes.
Over all of the losses.
Over my new body.
Over my new self.
Over my new life.

In the span of one night,
I blinked
and was gone.
In the span of one night,
I blinked
and was reborn.

ALMOST DYING BROUGHT ME HERE

I woke up from my surgeries
a different person.
I like this new me,
though some days the grief
is all-consuming and crippling.
But the ghosts aren't as loud anymore,
the darkness not as heavy.
Despite the missing and the dead,
despite the heartache and melancholy,
I'm learning to live.
After spending a lifetime
wanting to disappear,
almost dying
brought me here.
Alive,
bruised and scarred,
but here.

COMEDY OF HORRORS

The past few years
have been harder than expected.
(I always say that,
don't I?)

Burned home,
dead mother,
brain surgeries,
kidney surgery,
dead dog,
multiple diagnoses,
rehabilitation.
(Why am I keeping track of it all?)

It has become a joke of sorts,
a shitty comedy of horrors,
of everything I've endured
and how much longer
the sky will keep falling.
I've learnt not to make plans
or expect to see tomorrow
or the day after that.

I'm taking my life hour by hour,
letting go when I used to hold on.
Allowing myself to hope
for once in my life.
Letting myself live
after a lifetime
of wanting to disappear.

THE IRREVERSIBLE NATURE OF LIFE

In the span of one night,
everything I knew
was irrevocably changed.
I lost so much but I'm alive,
changed but still me.
I struggle
to speak,
to think,
to see,
but I remain,
steadfast and determined.
And despite the struggles,
I survived my worst days.
I will survive this too.

DROWN MYSELF IN SOFTNESS

The grief is always there,
just beneath my skin.
It comes in waves,
crashing and devouring,
waiting,
always waiting,
for a quiet moment to take me back,
under the memories and what-ifs.
To remembering
my mother is dead,
my dog is dead,
I almost died,
I'm forever changed,
and nothing will ever be the same.
I'm learning
to see through the sadness,
relieved I didn't drown
in the burdensome melancholy.
I'm trying to hope,
even if the grief is sometimes too heavy.
Allow myself a chance
to feel triumphant I survived,
to see past the murkiness of mourning,

to feel both stricken and thankful
I survived so many things
and came out hungrier for more.
So for once
I'm giving myself permission to feel
both the sharp edges of grief
and the softness of gratitude,
and be both
giving and selfish with myself.
The grief is always there,
waiting for its chance to pull me back under.
But now I'm going
to drown myself in softness,
give myself the grace and freedom
to simply be for once.

I'LL SURVIVE THESE SHARP EDGES BECAUSE I'M STUBBORN

In the past three years,
I lost my mother to cancer,
I lost my dog to old age,
I lost myself to illness.

My mother was eaten away from cancer.
My dog disappeared when I wasn't there.
My brain tried to erase me.

This year,
I'm trying to find myself,
to thrive in this new body
with this new brain
and these new eyes
in the space
I'm finally letting myself take up.

Last week,
the grief was crushing.
I was reminded how different I am now,
unable to move forward,
unwilling to accept the changes in me.

Yesterday,
there was grief.
So much grief that I'm not sure
I'll ever move past it.
Yet despite the crushing sadness,
there was gratitude and hope.
I'm so fucking grateful
for a second chance at living.

Today,
I can breathe through the grief.
Though crushing,
it is survivable.
The sadness and its sharp edges,
which niggle and erode and sting,
are no longer insurmountable.
My skin has survived
rough hands and sharper edges,
and the grief is just another edge
I can survive too.

And tomorrow,
I have to believe I'll survive the day.
Breathe through the fear of loss
and trust myself that I can survive
the darkness that tries to undo me.
Tomorrow I'll start again
with open hands and a giving heart.

SUNSHINE GIRL

During my rehabilitation,
my therapists commended me
on my good humour and upbeat
sunny attitude.
Saying that despite what I've endured,
I came out swinging
and hungry to devour life.

I once asked why was I being praised
for doing what I needed to do
to survive,
and I was told,

> "Not everyone wants to continue
> after what you've endured.
> Despite the crushing sadness,
> you've bloomed.
> And even grieving and facing the unknown,
> you've smiled and laughed and flourished."

UNENCUMBERED AND UNTETHERED

In every appointment
my doctor,
my specialist,
ask me for my medical history,
the medication I'm taking,
how my health is currently,
and what symptoms I'm exhibiting.

And suddenly,
I'm no longer me.
I'm there but not.
Half-girl and half-spectre.
Half-alive and halfway gone.

I'm words on a paper,
a problem to solve,
a topic for others to discuss.

There are days when I'm empty,
but moments when I know I'm more.
Then there are hours,
dark and choking,
when I can't move forward.

Can't find myself,
and not liking my reflection I see
in peoples' eyes.

I guess today is going to be
thick and heavy to wade through,
uncomfortable and chafing,
abrasive against my tender flesh.

But maybe tomorrow
I'll be able to find
the humour in my gloom,
at this comedic tragedy,
a horrific masterpiece.

I'll hang my skin above my bed,
clutch my bones in my hands,
and parade around
with my macabre trophies,
proud I survived
when I was expected to drown.

Hopeful that tomorrow
I'll be able to sew myself back together,
finally unencumbered and free.

THERE IS GRIEF IN LOSING

my dog,
my memories,
my vision,
my independence.

But there is also endless
and enduring happiness.

I'm alive.
I'm here.

I am.

I MAKE JOKES ABOUT MY VISION LOSS TO COPE

I lighten the heaviness in the air
by telling others
to stand in my blindspots,
so I don't have to see them
when I'm annoyed.

I laugh because the truth
is a raw edge against my skin,
some days more cutting
than bearable.

The vision loss is permanent,
my doctors tell me.
One of my eye specialists
listed a myriad of things
I'll no longer be able to do
because of my fading sight.

So I joke and hide behind
the laughter and smiles.
Sometimes the laughter
is honest and light,
but there are moments

when it's feigned and empty,
cloaking my insecurities and sadness.

In those moments,
I try not to let the changes in me
crunch on my bones,
holding steadfast on
to the deep gratitude
I still have some vision left.

Because if I remind myself
of everything I lost,
I'll drown in a tidal wave of grief,
and I'm not sure
I'll be able to survive it.

So I laugh
when the grief is too heavy,
when the sadness is too cutting,
when the unfairness of it all is too sharp.

And in my laughter and lightness,
I realize I can get through this:
the heaviness of grief
and the overwhelming changes in me.
I can live,
and I can thrive.

REMEMBERING THE LITTLE MOMENTS

I take photographs
of everything these days.
Pictures
of my outfits,
of food I've cooked and eaten,
of what I'm doing in that moment.
Snapshots of my life,
moments I collect
so I can try to remember them,
when my failing memory
will inevitably lose them.
When I look at these snapshots,
the sadness is suffocating,
but I am lightened by the gratefulness
of what I've survived and everything I have,
and I let myself fly away.

DESPITE

I feel selfish
for being ill,
for healing,
for recovering,
for focusing on myself.

I feel useless asking for help
to cook dinner,
to open doors,
to walk without falling.

I feel worthless
for being different,
for my vision loss,
for my failing memory.

I feel different
from how I think of myself,
from how I speak to myself,
from how I treat myself.

But today I feel light
despite the growing pains,
despite the uncomfortable days,
despite the loneliness.
Despite, despite, despite.

IN WHICH I AM GIVEN AN AWARD FOR MY COURAGE AND COMMENDED FOR MY POSITIVITY DURING MY REHABILITATION (OR) IN WHICH I'M A CONTRARY ASSHOLE

And I tell my therapist,

> *"I'm doing what I need to do*
> *to survive another day.*
> *How belittling it is feels to be given an award*
> *for trying to survive in my new body."*

But she tells me,

> *"Annie, it takes more than surviving*
> *when so many gave up.*
> *It takes resiliency to take up space*
> *and unapologetically live*
> *despite standing on the edge of life.*
> *It takes courage to simply be."*

After receiving my award,
I hid the glass sculpture in my closet.
It is a reminder of both
how far I've come
and how irrevocably I've changed.
Both a bruise and a kiss.

I'm proud and belittled,
honoured and hurt.
I did what I had to do to survive,
and yet,
I am proud I made a home
in this new body.

I'M TOO BORED TO REMAIN THE SAME

I'm happy I'm alive,
even if some days
I wonder why I survived,
when the grief is heavy,
and the sadness is crushing.
How ironic that after spending
a lifetime wanting to die,
I'm happy to be here.

LAUGHING TOO LOUDLY

When I think of the work
I still need to do in therapy
to heal and grow and thrive,
I want to go back to who I was before.
I grieve what I've lost,
mourn which will never be
and my dreams I have to let go.
I have to accept this new body
and its limitations,
move forward
regardless of wishing I could go back.
I have to learn to live
after spending a lifetime
cutting myself to pieces
to fit into spaces too small for me.
I'm saying goodbye to my old self,
and I'm no longer apologizing
for laughing too loudly.
I'm untethering myself
from what dares
try to hold me back.

IN THE LAST THREE YEARS

My home was lost to a fire,
and we had to leave
all we knew and had
in the middle of the night.

My mother was eaten by cancer,
and I stood vigil over her
as she succumbed to it
a few weeks later.

My dog of fourteen years,
who had been a lifeline
through my destructive madness,
died when I wasn't there.

I went to the hospital for a migraine
and woke up forever changed,
losing my memories and vision,
my independence and myself.

In the past year,
I've gained a newfound gratefulness
for those I love,

for everything I have,
for my life.

After spending a lifetime
wanting to implode and fade away,
I'm okay with being alive.

I still struggle with the grief
over all of these losses.
I'm still burdened
with the memory of who I used to be
and everything I left behind.

But I'm learning
to breathe through the heartbreak,
letting the sadness and happiness
wash over me in waves.

I remind myself I'm different now
and in my differentness,
I'm making a home for myself.

TINY LITTLE BURDENS

Their love,
little burdens in my pocket,
weighs me
down,
down,
down.

They want me to get better
and return to normal,
whatever the hell "normal" is.
They're unable to accept
I'm forever changed,
and forever different.

Even with my patchwork vision
and jigsaw brain,
they expect me to be
the Annie they used to know,
who I grieve for but don't miss.

These pebbles of grief,
tiny little burdens
lining my pocket,

are too heavy to carry,
rubbing me raw.

I move forward,
moving on when they try
to hold me back
with their grief-stained love.

I've outgrown
my old skin,
them,
me.

I've outgrown
and I'm flying away.

IN WHICH I'VE SAID "I LOVE YOU" MORE NOW THAN I'VE EVER HAD BEFORE

After losing
my mom,
my dog,
my health,
almost myself,

I'm scared,
terrified I'll lose more.

I used to be petrified
of my vulnerability
and letting others see
the love sewn on my sleeve.

But I'm no longer scared,
no longer anxious
of letting others in,
or of handing them pieces of me
and letting them see what is scrawled
on my heart.

HOW COMPLETELY I'VE CHANGED, HOW UTTERLY DIFFERENT I AM

My therapist says I'm vulnerable now
with this new brain of mine,
and it cuts
because it's true
because I still think I'm the old me
because I'm the only one changed
and on fast forward,
while everyone remains the same.

She says it's easy for people
to exploit me now
with my new personality
and I want to refute her,
argue that I'm unchanged
and untouchable,
but already I've been used,
already I've been hurt.

She tells me it's okay
to be different now,
and I tell her
I want to drown myself in softness,

finally let myself
laugh and feel and hope.
To live my life the way I choose
and allow myself to simply be.

I AM WHO I AM AND YET I AM NOT

In the span of three years
my home burned down,
my mother died,
my dog died,
I had two brain surgeries,
a kidney surgery,
gained too many new disorders,

and lost
my autonomy,
my memories,
myself.

Everything has changed
so irrevocably,
so drastically,
and yet,
nothing has changed at all.

Maybe only I've changed.
The only one moving forward
while everyone remains behind.
They try to hold me back

to when my health was steady,
to when I was predictable
and life was easier.

They're unaware of their grasping
gnarled fingers digging into my flesh
as they attempt to hold me back with them.

I used to feel drowned beneath the grief,
and changes,
and uncertainty,
but there is relief in the unknown,
because I am constantly transforming.

I am evolving amidst the chaos,
but there is also freedom in knowing
I am not who I was
last week
or yesterday
or who I'll be
tomorrow.

MOVING ON, MOVING FORWARD

I.
I spent most of my life wanting to die,
more than twenty-two years
tearing myself to pieces.
I was an obsessive people-pleaser
who tried to find herself in sharp edges
and men with sharper hands.

II.
Now that I've tasted illness
and stood on the peripherals of death,
I realized I've been missing from my own life.
Trying to rebuild my shelter,
restitching my skin back together,
layer by layer.
I want to find myself,
whoever the hell I am now.

III.
After years of self-destructive madness,
years spent wanting to disappear,
I'm here.
I'm alive,

and I can finally breathe
past the sadness and anger.
I'm able to breathe
without the burning need
to dig and hurt and bleed.
I can move forward,
unfettered and free.

MY STUBBORN THRIVING HEART

Trembling hands and unsteady gait.
Lost vision and forgotten memories.
They can't see past
my disabilities and challenges.

They can't see my humanity,
too nervous to come near
my gnashing teeth and biting laughter.

So I let them believe what they see,
and thinking I'm less than
because I'm different.
Let them dehumanize and characterize me
as dumb or stupid or simple.
Their words can't hurt me.
Their hands are sharp when they touch me
but my tongue is sharper.
Let them believe
I'm different and weird and dumb.
Let them believe what they see
because I'm untouchable.

I've survived through hell

and back and came out
thirsty and unrelenting,
hungry and alive.

I'm singed from anger's flames
and sore from crawling
through lonely madness.
But I'm here and I'm alive.

Their words will never reach me,
their image of me can't confine me,
and I will not live by their definitions
of who I should be.
So I'll raise my glass at dinner tonight
and toast my thriving heart.

GREAT. YET ANOTHER POEM ON MY SUDDEN WILL TO LIVE AND SHINING GRATITUDE

I guess I could write another poem
on triumphing over death
and on my newly found desire to live.
In which I survived hell and back
and came out swinging.

Or maybe I could write of trying to live
in this new body in this new life.
I worry words will lose their meaning
if I write I only had a day or two left
to me if I hadn't had surgery.
Or of how on most days,
I'm too tired
to eat and struggle to speak,
and I still bump into walls and spill things
because of my loss of sight and coordination.

But I'm tired of thinking about
what I left behind,
almost dying,
my new body,
my new life.

I move forward,
grateful to be alive
but choking on the burdensome truth
that the price was steep.

This is the end of the poem
in which I promise I'll try
to hold onto the lightness,
and carry it with me
wherever I go.

ON THE DAYS WHEN THE GRIEF IS TOO HEAVY TO CARRY

Some days are harder than others
and when I don't like this new me,
when I can't stand who I am now,
I stay in my room,
not leaving my bed.

Those are the days when I wonder
why I survived.
What is left of me.
if there is anything left at all?

It's hard to breathe on those days,
harder to wake up
after having lost so much.
But I survived my darkest days.
I survived surgery after surgery,
waking up when doctors thought I wouldn't.

I'm forever changed,
and I am no longer recognizable.
I have peeled my skin from my body and regrew,
despite the pains and aches of yesterdays.
I'm learning to laugh,

to breathe through heaviness
and see through the melancholy.

For the first time in my life,
I'm learning gratefulness.
I'm grateful I'm alive,
grateful for those I love,
and despite all I've lost,
grateful to be here.

I GUESS MY TWO BRAIN SURGERIES ARE BLESSINGS IN DISGUISE

I'm more content than I've ever been.
Happy even.

I'm finally comfortable in my skin,
no longer wishing I could rip myself
to shreds.

I'm grateful to be alive,
even if I've spent most of my life
wanting to disappear.

I'm present,
even if I grieve for who I was
and what I've lost.

I'm here.

I HAD SO MANY PLANS FOR LAST YEAR (THE LIES I TELL MYSELF)

I was going to publish two more books
(I guess I'm delusional)

I was going to take my dog on longer walks
(she's gone now)

I was going to work towards a Master's degree
(I can barely finish a novel these days)

I was going to enjoy every blissful moment of life
(I'm drowning in bitter grief)

Then my body tried to kill me,
and I desperately fought to live
(ironic,
for a girl who spent a lifetime
wanting to die)

I did a year of rehabilitation,
relearning to walk independently
and speak coherently,
rebuilding myself
piece by painful piece,

struggling to accept my new life
(I don't miss who I was,
but I miss the comfort of what I knew)

These goals are too high to reach these days
(I'm not sure if I can carry
their weight much longer)

I'm trying to rebuild myself,
missing pieces along the way,
trying to make a home in my new body
(if I can keep myself
from drowning in the grief)

Even here,
I can't find an ending to this poem
(I hate saying goodbye,
even if it rots in my hands)

I want to weave hope in these words
(but I'm a hopeless asshole today)

so I let myself sink
into the unbearable heaviness of sadness,
let myself drown and tell myself
I can always begin anew tomorrow.

THE TIME IT TAKES

Gone are the days when I remembered
people's faces and names,
where I was and who I was.

There are some days I miss the old me,
who felt invincible and was ignorant
of the ephemerality of the body
and fleeting life.

I miss waking up bitter and biting,
gnashing my teeth for a sliver of kindness.
I miss my raw edges and sharp smiles,
my razor eyes and cutting words.

Now I wake up every morning the lost girl,
a girl without a name,
with smiles that come too easily
and who hugs too tightly.

So I tumble between
wanting to slip away
and this new desire
to breathe and live and flourish.

Most days I welcome the unknown
and the days ahead of me
with open arms and eager hands.

I am changed,
my body different and future uncertain,
but I've made a home here
and my life is my own.
So I let go of my past,
move forward
and be.

THE UNFURLING

I need to stop comparing myself
to who I was before,
to who I was last year
and the year before that.

Because nothing is the same anymore,
and comparing the present
to what is behind me
does nothing but flay me open
and rub salt into my tender flesh.

It's just another way to hurt myself
and after spending a lifetime
cutting myself to pieces,
I'm tired of being a rag doll,
misshapen and twisted.

I'm learning what it means
to like myself,
to honour my triumphs,
to not drown in the sadness when it comes.

It'll take time
to feel comfortable in my skin,
to not tear myself apart,
to smile freely and unfettered.

Today isn't one of those days,
and I'm learning that it's okay
because I know this heaviness won't last forever.
I'm learning to release the darkness
I've held onto for so long,
letting myself feel both
the sharpness and the softness.

I'm giving myself space
to simply breathe,
permission to unfurl
and become whoever the hell
I want to be.

MY BODY—THE BASTARD—TRIED TO KILL ME BUT I WON

My body,
what should have been a safe haven,
became a traitor and a prison.

I spent a lifetime wanting to destroy
this body of mine,
but in the span of a few days,
I almost succumbed
to it trying to erase me.

I can't live in my anger anymore
because what is the point
in making a home in it?
What's the point
when there's endless sadness
I wade through,
so thick I struggle
to breathe sometimes.

If only I had my old rage
I used to thrive in,
maybe then I could feel something
other than grief.

Being gone but being here.
Being me but not.
Being lost but found.

So I sit with my sadness
and wish I could rage.
Rage against
the unfairness of it all,
my new life,
and my body—
this fucker who betrayed and saved me.

But I'm tired.
Tired of being sad.
Tired of the darkness.
Tired of my old self.
Tired of being tired.
Tired, tired, tired.

Where do I go from here?
Who will I decide to be?
Who will I become?

Maybe my body,
in trying to kill me,
it saved me.
Maybe in a fucked-up way,
my body gave me a reset.

Though some days
are heavier than others
and the light is harder to find,
I'll take it.
I'll take the reset
and plant myself here
and grow.

Grow into
someone new,
someone alive,
someone in love with life.

IN WHICH I'VE MOVED ON

This woman who shares my blood,
has made me feel more uncomfortable
in my new skin
than even my darkest insecurities
have ever done.

She tells me I look *"retarded and dumb,"*
lies to others about my memory
and steals from me.

I try not to chew on the bitterness
that the one who I thought
loved and protected me,
is the one who has hurt me irrevocably.
Her attention is conditional,
she's only present when she can
use and take and steal.

She weaves lies so perfectly
everyone believes them to be truths.
It used to sting and chafe and ache,
and I spent years
wanting to defend myself.

But now I don't care.
I don't care about the lies.
I don't care about them believing her.
I don't care about her.

I'm free now.
Free from her and her gnarled fingers
and twisted words.
I'm untethered and for the first time,
I can finally breathe.

COFFEE AND BITTER TRUTHS

My friend told me over coffee one day
that because of my brain injury,
I'm vulnerable now,
more than I ever was before.

At first there was devastation
and wishing I could disappear.
I wanted to apologise and self-destruct,
reverting back to who I used to be,

But her words sunk into my marrow,
raw and full of truths.
It took me days to admit to myself
I am more vulnerable than before,
days to finally be able
to look at my reflection
and tell myself
there is nothing wrong with me.

I am not weak for needing help.
I am not fragile for being different.
I am not broken for being changed.

THE DICHOTOMY OF BEING HERE BUT MISSING

I'm starting to forget
more and more these days,
and I crack and break and cry.

I grieve for what I was forced
to leave behind
and ache on the days
when the sadness
is a struggle to carry.

But I can still laugh
when I'm able to remind myself
I survived and I am here.

Instead of holding onto
my sharp edges and shadowed grief,
instead of telling myself
I'm lost and faceless,
I give myself space and kindness
and wrap myself in tender softness.

I'm curious to see
where I go from here.
I'm excited to unfurl
and bloom into whoever
I'll become.

DESPITE THE VISION LOSS, I CAN SEE CLEARER NOW THAN BEFORE

My brain's drama
has irreparably changed who I am.
But it has also changed the people in my life.
It is a sieve filtering
those who are genuine
and treat me the same as before.
But it forces me to see
the ones who are condescending
and treat me with fragility.

Almost losing myself
simplified my life,
stripping it bare,
bringing me here.

Finally I'm able to distinguish
the love from the hollow words.
See those who support and sincerely care,
and those who gnash their teeth,
eagerly waiting for me to falter.

I'm learning to disregard
those who act mightier

because they are unchanged,
while I struggle to remember
how to live.

I'm learning to let go,
reminding myself
I'm free to move on.

IN WHICH I COVER MY HOME IN STICKY NOTES

My home is covered in sticky notes,
reminding me of basic things
I used to take for granted
before the brain surgeries.
Turn off the stove.
Lock the door when I leave.
What to eat if I'm hungry.

I speak slower these days,
struggle to see past the tip of my nose.
It's surreal how deeply I've changed
and how different my life is now.

When I can't breathe through the grief,
I let myself break
and give myself space to simply be.
But I don't hold onto the sadness anymore,
no longer making a home
in my darkened edges.

I'm able to feel the sunshine on my skin,
laugh and smile without
the burning need to tear myself to shreds.

I don't feel the obsession
with wanting to drown myself
under the waves of sadness
as I used to.

How far I've come.
How deeply I've changed.
I can look at myself in the mirror
without wanting to gnash on my bones.

I can see me,
who survived so much
and is finally free
to live as I choose.

AM I AN ASSHOLE?

for being annoyed
when they try to hold my arm
thinking I'm unable
to walk on my own

for feeling resentful
when they compare my past self
to who I am now

for wanting to go back
to what is behind me
just so I could say goodbye
one more time
to those I lost

for leaving behind
the ones who hurt me to rot

for creating a new self
and a new life

for finally allowing myself
the chance to live and heal
and move on.

In the Mourning

*THE CYCLICAL NATURE OF BEING
SAD AND BEING HAPPY*

Where does the sadness end
and the joy begin?

WHEN?

When will I feel like I can breathe
in this new body?
When will I feel comfortable
with myself?

When will I know myself
as I once did before,
with my sharp tongue
and my rough edges?

When will my life
feel like mine again?
When will my body
feel like home?

STUCK IN THE MIDDLE

I am here
in the space between
giving up and giving in,
self-love and self-loathing,
self-acceptance and self-rejection.

I am here
alive but wanting to go back.
Back to when I was half-existing,
hating life but hating myself more.

I miss the madness
and the comfort it brought me,
the familiarity of the darkness,
and the ghosts tethered to my bones.

Yet I'm glad
I am here.

Yesterday,
today,
and the day after that.

And in the space between
who I was
and who I'm becoming,
I breathe.

Alive.

Broken and grieving,
but alive.

2024

I've spent more than 30 years
wanting to die,
trying to find myself
and not liking what I found.
Barely able to breathe,
only surviving in my skin.
Taking everything that I was
and all that I had for granted,
not realizing how quickly
it could all slip away.
And in a blink of a second,
I had to restart.
Go back to the beginning.
Relearn who I am
and how to live in this new body,
in this new life of mine.
So I begin.
The first year
where I start again,
begin anew.
The first year
of my new forever.

The first year
of me.

GROWING PAINS

I used to eat wormwood for dinner
and tried to find peace
in my body with sharp edges.
I made a home in my self-loathing,
comfort in wanting to disappear.
I found the chaos comfortable,
liked being the fucked-up girl,
more gnashing teeth than smiles.
Twisted and bitter,
hurt and devastated.

But I no longer miss
the darkness,
the hurt,
the sadness.
I don't miss digging around in my body
trying to find peace
in my self-loathing and grief.

I used to be terrified
of losing myself.
Would I become a Stepford girl
with plastic smiles and shallow laughter

if I let go of my darkness?

So I clung to what I knew,
despite the heaviness slowly eating me alive.

Then I fell ill and woke up,
two brain surgeries later.

I'm different now.
Brittle smiles turned
glittered and honest.
I'm comfortable in my skin,
for the first time in my life.
The loudness in my head
calming to a quiet lull.

I don't shy away
from touch or feign warmth
when people tell me they care.

I'm invested.
I'm all in.
I'm eager to jump headfirst into life,
with its rough edges and uncertainty.

I spent my life
wanting to become a ghost,
digging for stillness in my skin,
trying to starve myself to be worthy.

But I'm okay now.
I'm finally able to breathe
through the melancholic gloom.
Able to live in my body
without wanting to strip
my skin from my bones,

no longer consumed with self-loathing.

Venomous and twisted little doll
turned eager girl
with bright smiles and soft hands.
How funny that I had to stand
on the edge of almost dying
to be grateful my body is still here.

I used to be terrified of losing myself
to the sunshine
if I let go of the darkness.
Who would I be
without the melancholy and my shadows?

But I'm still here.
Different and changed,
growing pains and all.

I'm still me.
Even if I'm unsure
of who I am most days.
But I'm learning
to like myself,
to live,
to be.

Now I feast on hope for breakfast,
remind myself I've survived hell
and back
and back again.

I'm here,
scarred and misshapen,
different and changed.
But I'm here.

I'M TOO IMPATIENT TO BE A SAINT

In the span of three years
I lost my home to a fire,
my mother died,
my dog died,
I almost joined them,
I forgot myself.

In the span of sixteen months
I moved back to my rebuilt home,
I'm relearning to make a home
in my new body,
in this new life of mine.

It took a lifetime of struggling
to keep myself afloat,
and I know it'll take me
the rest of my life
to learn to come alive.

LOVING WHOLLY

I'm no longer afraid of the ghosts
lurking just outside of my peripheral vision
and the darkness I'd once made a home in
for most of my life.

Now I'm terrified of loss
and love without a home.
I'm scared of loving and losing,
wondering what to do
with all this love
when they're gone.

I'm scared of waking up one day
and my loved ones being dust
like the ones before them.
I'm terrified of their ghosts
and tasting their absences in my life.

I'm trying to
live despite the fear,
laugh despite the heaviness,
love despite the grief.

I'm reminding myself I can't love
while holding onto the fear of loss and grief.
I have to love wholly and freely
and fearlessly.

THESE DAYS

I forget names and places,
can't remember which direction
is left and which way is right.
Faces are barely recognizable
and what I did yesterday,
or even an hour ago,
is hopelessly forgotten.

A few days ago,
I couldn't remember how to use the shower.
A few days ago,
I couldn't remember how to boil water.
A few days ago,
I couldn't remember when I last ate.

I joke about my forgetfulness
because if I don't laugh,
I'll drown in an ocean of grief.

This is my reality.
This is who I am now.
I'm moving forward,
learning to find myself
in my new life.

I'm letting the happiness and sadness coexist.
I'm allowing myself the chance to feel the sun.
For the first time in my life,
I'm letting myself bloom.

BEING PRESENT

It still doesn't feel real.
How close to death I was.
How changed I am.
How different my life is now.

So much of what I lost,
I'll never get back.
I think I'll wake up tomorrow
and be back to who I was
and the life I took for granted.

But then I wake up
and I'm still here.
With a shaved head and missing memories,
misshapen skull and trembling limbs,
puzzle-pieced vision and unsteady gait.

I'm utterly and painfully thankful
I'm still breathing,
even if I'm halfway missing.
Half a girl and half a ghost,
here but unsure of where I am.

Maybe there'll come a day
when I feel at home
in this new body,
in my new life.

Maybe there'll be a day
when the grief isn't as cutting
and I'll be able to breathe
past the mourning.

When I'll be comfortable in my skin,
allow myself space to unfurl
and live.

THIS IS THE FIRST POEM I'VE FINISHED IN A YEAR AND I'M GOING TO CELEBRATE WITH ICE CREAM

I haven't been able to finish
a poem in over a year,
haven't been able to complete
the half-finished painting
leaning against my bedroom wall.
Both are mocking reminders
of how deeply I've changed.

I'm relieved the words
haven't completely abandoned me.
But still,
I struggle.

Some days
this hollowness hurts more
than the scar tissue on my head,
having always needed words
more than air.
I stay in bed and wish I could go back.
Back to when I took life for granted,
and the words came easily,
slipped from my fingers
like sand through an hourglass.

And other days are tempered
with a deep gratefulness I'm alive.
Even though it cost me so much.
Even though words have to be torn
from my skin now.
Even though it's no longer easy to speak or write.
Even though, even though, even though.

Who would've thought
I would turn into this sunshine girl
with endless laughter
and pockets filled with gratitude?

WHAT I'M TOLD

They say I should be kind to myself
for being changed,
for healing,
for this new me.

They say I should be more understanding
towards myself
for the days when I can't remember
the simplest of things,
and being unable to see like I used to.

They say it will take time to heal,
and there'll be a day when the grief
won't be as cutting.

They say I'll be able to breathe now,
after a lifetime of drowning,
and I've been given a second chance
if I grasp it.

And I will.

Despite the pinpricks and loss,
I'm going to come alive.
I'm going to unfurl.
I'm going to flourish.

THE BITTERSWEETNESS OF LIFE

Despite the illnesses,
the changes around me
and the losses,
I'm grateful to be alive.
But with this new lightness,
the darkness still remains.
Not suffocating or debilitating,
but still present.
Waiting and lurking
but survivable.

IN WHICH I'M A SARCASTIC ASSHOLE, PART I

Thank you for pointing out
how different I am now
in a disparagingly biting tone.

Thank you for laughing
when I become injured or fall
because of my loss of sight
and coordination.

Thank you for making jokes
about my newly developed epilepsy
and how I could hurt myself
by having a seizure.

Thank you for taking photographs
of me during my private
and vulnerable moments,
then sharing them without my consent.

Thank you for taking advantage
of my memory loss
and stealing from me.

Thank you for gaslighting me
and speaking to me
as though I were too dim-witted
to understand.

Thank you for everything
you've done for me
and for removing yourself from my life.

I've never been as happy to see
the end of us as I am now.
I wish you all the best.

Fuck you.

FORGIVING MYSELF FOR A LIFETIME OF SELF-IMMOLATION

I spent a lifetime drowning in self-loathing,
wishing I could float away and disappear,
vanishing into the air.
Spent my days disgusted
with my skin and bones,
unable to look at my reflection
without wanting to tear myself to shreds.

Doctors said I only had hours,
maybe a day or two,
left in me.
I woke up from the surgeries,
finally comfortable in my body.
How funny almost dying
woke me up from a lifetime
of slumbered darkness.

For once,
I no longer want to tear myself to shreds.
And now,
sixteen months into my recovery,
I'm learning to like myself.

I'm learning to forgive myself
for having spent a lifetime
tearing myself apart
and dissecting myself in hopes
of finding my self-worth.
And forgive my traitorous body
for trying to erase me
from my own life.

Now I have the rest of my life
to heal
and grow
and thrive.

HOW TO SURVIVE THE ENDURING GRIEF

I.
Overnight I lost
my dog,
my memories,
my ability to walk steadily,
to remember,
to move without trembling,
the feeling in my feet,
half of my vision.

II.
I closed my eyes as Annie,
the venomous and twisted girl,
and woke up,
unsure of who I was
and who I'd become.
Most days I swing between
unending gratitude I'm not dead
and the drowning grief
at all I've lost.

IV.
I'm told I should be grateful
I survived.
I'm told I should look around
and breathe easy
because I'm still alive.

V.
I am utterly thankful,
but still,
there is grief.
So much grief
that most days,
I don't know which way is up
and which way is down.

VI.
It's crushing and yet,
it's survivable.
Excruciating
but never insurmountable.

IN WHICH I DECIDE TO GIVE LIVING A TRY

Isn't it ironic
I've spent most of my life
wanting to die?
But when I woke up after my first surgery,
and on the edge of vanishing,
I wasn't ready to go.
So I clung on,
despite my youthful dreams
of being a ghost.
I clung on and decided
to give living a try.

DEFIANTLY BEGINNING ANEW

Speaking slowly
as if I don't understand words,
raising their voices
as if I'm hard of hearing.

The condescending smiles
and hollow laughter,
the pitying looks
and patronizing words
of false comfort.

I'm sure they mean well,
but good intentions are meaningless
when they try to drown me
in their counterfeit kindness.
They think they are good people
for helping poor and pathetic me.
They think they are kind
when they are quietly cruel.

Some days it's suffocating and abrasive,
rubbing me raw and sore.
Other days it's gasoline

I douse myself in and ignite,
being reborn and beginning afresh.

I'm hungrier than I've ever been,
burning so bright I blind them.
I'm disentangling myself,
finally free from their gnarled grasps,
unfurling and taking up space.
I'm unapologetically coming alive,
fiercely and defiantly
and freely.

BEFORE AND NOW

I wouldn't have expected
this sudden desire to live,
having spent more than half my life
wanting to disappear.
To float away.
To be only a memory.

I had always wanted to be no one
other than the fuck-up,
the bipolar girl with gnashing teeth
and uncombed hair.

After wanting to die for so long,
I don't know what it means to live
fully and completely.
But I'm trying.
Trying to come alive
and embrace this new body,
my new self.

Before I didn't think I could go on
without my dog,
without my vision,

without my memory.

And now I have,
despite my new life,
despite the challenges it brings,
despite myself.

I'm embracing what it means
to come alive in this space
I've carved for myself.
I'll be the unkempt girl
with wild eyes and claws for hands,
who lives completely,
no longer afraid
of her own shadow,
or the light peeking through the cracks.
The girl who wants to swallow the sky
and dance in the sunshine.

Before
I spent my life waiting to die,
and now
I'm going to live.

GROWING A GARDEN IN MY BONES

I courted death my whole life,
wishing I could slip away into nothingness
and no longer be.

I spent so long in this limbo,
halfway between
wanting to die and wanting to come alive.
I made a home in this self-made cage
of self-destructive melancholy
and unrelenting madness.

But now after almost dying,
after actually being on the precipice
of only having a day or two left in me,
I'm learning to accept I'm okay with being alive
and to be content with my present self.

I'm finally living this life of mine.

HOW TO GET WHIPLASH BY MOVING FORWARD WHILE MISSING THE PAST

For most of my rehabilitation,
I told myself I had to heal
so I could go back to who
I used to be.

But on the first anniversary
of falling ill and my surgeries,
I'm faced with the bitter realization.
I'm no longer that Annie,
the twisted and furious girl.
No longer are there days
when I want to slip away
and become a phantom.

I told myself daily while healing,
that it was only a matter of time
before I could be that sad girl again,
convinced I would be the same
I had been before the surgeries.

But I realized yesterday
there is no turning back.
This is who I am now.

This is my new life.
My new body.
My new everything.
How freeing.
How suffocating.

I had convinced myself
to be patient and wait
for the shadows to return.
But I know now
they won't possess me
and make a home in my bones
like before.

I've changed.
Despite missing the comfort
of the darkness,
I'm finally learning to embrace
the lightness.

IN WHICH I'M A SARCASTIC ASSHOLE, PART II

Thank you for telling me to be kind to myself
and give myself space to grow.

Thank you for telling me to be happy I'm alive,
despite losing so much
because at least I still have my life.

Thank you for telling me to go for walks,
dismissing my struggles with my vision loss
and disorientation.

Thank you for speaking over me,
negating how I'm feeling
and dismissing my struggles.

Thank you for trying to take over my life.
What would I do without you?

IN THE PAST THREE YEARS I'VE

lost my home to a fire
stood vigil over my mother as she died
had two brain surgeries and a kidney surgery to live
lost my dog while I wasn't there
lost vision and independence
lost my ability to remember and speak coherently
almost lost myself.

And despite it all,
I'm here.
For the first time in my life,
I'm happy I'm alive.

Even with all the loss,
I'm happy to be here.

HOW CONTRARY I'VE BECOME

I always dreamt of one day
coming alive and flourishing,
proudly taking up space and blooming.
And it took losing all I knew
to bring me here.

I was a butterfly
torn from the cocoon.
My salvation—
a bloody catastrophe.
A cruel metamorphosis.

Despite wanting
to hold onto all I knew,
and wishing I could remain
a bitter and hollow spectre,
I tore the old from my skin
and grew.

Despite the melancholy,
I'm blossoming.

IN ALL THE WAYS, IN EVERY WAY

I broke down earlier
in the middle of the kitchen,
sink full of suds and dirty dishes,
suffocating on the insurmountable grief
heavy in my gut.

This is it.
This is the new me.
I won't improve,
and I won't ever return
to who I was before.

So I cried
for the dreams I had to let go,
for the realization that I am completely changed,
for the days when I forget who I am,
for realizing I can't ever go back,
for everything I left behind,
for all that I lost.

Despite trying to move forward,
the grief remains,
unrelenting and enduring.

I don't know which way is up
and which way is down anymore.
Don't know
who I am,
where I'm going,
what life holds for me.

I don't know,
but I'm trying to remind myself
there is freedom in the unknown.
And for the first time in my life,

I'm finally free.
In all ways
and in every way,
I'm free.

IN WHICH I'M GRATEFUL TO THE GLENROSE HOSPITAL FOR MY REHABILITATION BUT I'M MOVING ON

I was nervous to be discharged
from my rehabilitation program,
where I spent almost a year in.
Relearning
to be independently mobile again,
to speak coherently,
to navigate with my new vision,
to teach myself ways to work
around my memory loss.

But I was officially discharged last Friday.
There wasn't anything more
the therapists could help me with
on my journey of recovery.

I thought I'd be scared to be on my own,
afraid to navigate the world
in my new body.

But I'm okay now.

I'm curious about what life holds for me
and who I'll become.

I'm eager to breathe
without the suffocating sadness,
excited to taste the colours around me.

So I take a step forward
and another
and another.

For once,
this body feels like home.
Finally,
this life feels like my own.

COMEDIC TRAGEDY

I make terrible jokes
about almost dying,
lost vision,
and a failing memory.

But if I can't laugh about my life,
a comedic horror story,
then why bother collecting moments at all?
If I can't tell people I love them
when I almost slipped away,
then why bother collecting
their smiles in photographs?

I laugh
because life is sometimes too dark.
I love
because I almost lost it all.

After spending a lifetime
tearing myself to pieces,
I'm finally giving myself
a chance to live.

LIGHTING MYSELF ON FIRE SO I CAN FLOAT AWAY

I'm learning to embrace the laughter
amidst the heaviness.
Accepting my shifting priorities
and diverging dreams.
Despite my vision loss,
I can finally see myself.
Despite the weight of sadness,
I feel the lightness in me.
Once tethered by the grief,
I am now unburdened and free.

THE RESILIENCY OF WEEDS

It has been hard to come to terms
with what I've endured,
and all of the changes
I've gone through,
with who I am now.

Sometimes it's hard and crushing
and other moments I'm blossoming.
A cycle of acceptance and denial,
a 'rinse and repeat'.

It'll come in waves
and always be a presence in my life.
But I know it won't be as consuming
as it once was.

I'm learning to breathe through the heaviness,
my skin thickening against
the sharp edges of these growing pains.
I struggle
and sometimes,
hope is cutting and cruel.

But in my struggles,
I remind myself
I'd rather be a weed
growing through the cracks in the concrete,
than a flower wilting in a rainstorm.

THE UNRAVELING

Having a brain injury
doesn't make me less
than anyone else.
I'm just as
worthy and deserving
as everyone.

But now I am both
bitterness and sugary sweet,
cutting and soft,
twisted and untangled.
Acerbic words and warm hands.

I am changed and unchanged.
Annie,
the venomous girl.
Annie,
the sunshine girl.

I used to care how others treated me,
wanting to tell them
to fuck off and let me be.
But now I find humour

in their attempts
to wrap me in their hollow compassion.

No longer do I place myself
in their hands,
or think of their words as truths.

I'm learning to stand on my own,
and use my voice I've buried
for most of my life.

I'm becoming,
despite the uncertainty,
I'm unfurling.

I'M A GREEDY JERK

I'm alive.
I'm here.
I've been given a second chance
and I'm going to take it
with both hands.
Wholly,
fully
and greedily.

Giving Thanks

ACKNOWLEDGEMENTS AND THANKS

I am keenly aware that I would not be where I am today if it were not for the many people I have met these past few years. I owe many thanks to them.

To my editor, Misti; thank you for your constant care, compassion, and attention to my work over the years we've worked together. It's wild to know you've been with me on this journey since my very first book.

Dr. Sankar, there aren't enough words to say how eternally grateful I am to you and for your care during my time at the University of Alberta Hospital. Simply put, thank you for saving my life and giving me a second chance. I'll always be eternally grateful to you.

Huge thank you to the staff at the University of Alberta Hospital who helped in my care, and thank you to everyone involved during my recovery since then.

Thank you to everyone I've met along the way who has helped me during my illnesses, recovery, and rehab journey.

To my brain: nice try, dickwad. Thanks but no thanks.

To everyone involved in my rehabilitation at the Glenrose Rehabilitation Hospital, here comes the long part, so brace yourselves.

Thank you, Mary, for your compassion and humour during my rehab. You knew when to challenge me, when to motivate me, and when to make me laugh. You cared about my recovery and inspired me, and I'll always be thankful.

Dan. Well, well, well. I bet you miss me bugging you in group. Let's be honest, I know you do because I'm a gift and pleasure to be around. You're welcome. But in all seriousness, thank you for everything you've done for me (whether it was making me lift weights or play those nerve-racking and challenging games), I'll forever be thankful to you.

Danica, I bet you miss me, my humour, and my humility. It must be hard now not having someone as humble as I was around. I guess I'll say thank you for helping me in my rehab. But honestly, thank you for motivating and supporting me in group, for always making me laugh even when I wanted to give up (I still stand by making myself have a seizure so I don't have to do anymore weightlifting though), and most of all, thank you for your care and compassion. (This is why you're top-tier—just keep that on the down-low though.) Above all, let's both stay humble.

Paige, thank you for your humour, your 'truth bombs' and your compassion. I still have those sticky notes you gave me, and though my memory is iffy, I remember them and the mantras we came up with. I'm still practicing what I learnt during our sessions, and I'm forever grateful.

Heather, I'm so thankful for your help and motivation during our PT sessions. I remember before PT with you, I struggled to go up stairs independently, and walking and navigating my surroundings on my own. It hasn't even been two years and I'm in awe of how far I've come and I'm keenly aware that I owe so much of that to you. Please know I'll forever be thankful to you and our sessions. P.S. Yes, I'm still working on my posture!

Alicia, I remember struggling to hold conversations (and even with speaking coherently) when I first started our sessions together. I've come along way since then and I'm acutely aware that this is because of you and your help. Our sessions challenged me and I loved every minute of them. You supported and motivated me, made me laugh when I needed the lightness, and helped me become confident in speaking and holding conversations again. Thank you so much for your dedication and care.

Cindy, thank you for everything you did for me during my time at Glenrose. During my recovery, I was apprehensive and anxiously worried when (or 'if') I'd ever be able to create again. Now I'm painting and writing again, I'm doing yoga, and I plan on doing way more in the near future. Not only did you help me find my creativity and passion again, but you also made me excited to be involved in activities and the world around me. This book exists because I was inspired to return to writing, and you were a large factor in that, so thank you.

Janine, thank you for your support during our sessions. I learnt so much from you, and I'm constantly excited and inspired by the world around me and this burning desire to paint and create art. Thank you for your kindness, support, and compassion during our sessions.

Ava and Paula, thank you for everything you both taught me during our memory group. You both showed me support, compassion, and care. I learnt so much from you both and I still utilize what I was taught during group. I'm utterly thankful to you both.

To everyone at the Glenrose, thank you. Thank you for the kindness, understanding, and empathy I was shown during my rehabilitation. I felt seen and heard, and I was treated with dignity. I'm undone and forever grateful.

My apologies if I didn't name-drop you. (Please insert a memory loss joke here.) Every single person involved in my rehabilitation greatly impacted me. I'm not saying this lightly, but I am changed because of all of you. Every one of you helped me grow and reclaim myself and I'm touched and forever grateful to you all and the Glenrose.

Gina, I know this isn't ice cream, but I hope it will suffice as a thank-you. It's been years since you've been sharing your "Ginaisms" with me and I'm forever appreciative and thankful for that. (I'll make t-shirts with them one day.) You've known both versions of me: the 'before brain drama Annie' and this new one. You've also seen me in my most darkest and gruesome moments. I know you're going to say I saved myself, but we both know you had a huge role in that. Thank you for being such a fantastic listener, advice-giver, life-sharer, and overall person. I'm forever grateful.

Bô, thank you for always being there for me, for being such a great papa, and overall being a pretty cool person. Though I don't tell you any of that often. These past sixteen months have been wild and I'm glad to have you here with me during all of it. Though I do have to say, huge sorry for all of the brain drama and health scares. Oh, and big whoops for that one time I had that seizure while you were driving—my bad. But seriously, thank you, Bô. I'm so lucky to have you in my life. Love you.

Friends, if you've made it this far, don't worry. This part is for you. Thank you for your support and love during all of this drama (sorry for not telling you I was in the hospital) and for being supportive, treating me the same as before, and for your humour. Absolute 10/10.

Tawnie, I don't even know where to begin. I'm struggling right now to write this (I don't want to write pages of mush) because I am so undone and grateful to you, our friendship, and your wisdom. The shit we've been through together has been wild, right? And if I had to go through it all again (I seriously hope not though), I'd still choose you to be my ride-or-die. You're funny, smart, and kick-ass, and I'm so lucky and thankful to have you in my life. Thank you and love you, girl.

Mackenzie, thank you for being such an amazing friend and person. We've known each other for years. (Let's not count how long and 'age' ourselves, okay?) After all of these years, I still consider myself lucky to both know you and have you in my life. Also, sorry for not telling you I was in the hospital; it must've been a shock. That time is fuzzy but I do remember you there with me, and despite the crushing pain in my head, I was so happy that day. Thank you and love you.

Meghan, I'm not sure if I should be mushy or make jokes; let's see if I can find the perfect balance. Thank you for knowing when to laugh with me, when to let me cry, and for listening and supporting me. From the very beginning of this brain nonsense, you've never treated me differently and I'm utterly grateful to you for that. We've known each other for a long time (ew, we're growing old) and you've seen me at my darkest and now lightest, and you still treat me with grace and love. You've always been a fantastic person, and I consider myself lucky to know you. Love you.

Mr. and Mrs. Sturdy, thank you for raising two amazing and smart daughters, thank you for always being there for me, and thank you for sharing your wisdom and love during my hardest moments. You've always been so supportive and loving, and not once have you treated me differently, and I'm so grateful to you both for that. Thank you so much for being amazing and genuine. I consider myself lucky to know you both and have you in my life.

Thank you to the 'A-team' for helping keep me sane while we worked together. We were hilarious, invincible, and yes, very cool.

Aylish, I'm not saying we made a perfect team...but...we did. You made misery bearable. You were hilarious, supportive, and I loved every moment with you. While I miss you and wish you were back here with us, I'm happy you've made a great life for yourself in B.C.

Arielle, even with my memory issues, I still remember the first day we met (I was awkward as hell, but you were so genuine and warm), and even after all of these years, you remain just as amazing and loving. You inspire me to be a better and kinder person. Thank you for being a great human and greater friend.

Arsalan, you know some of my shady shit, and you're still

here. Joking aside, I'm lucky to consider you a friend. You're funny, kind, and supportive. I'm constantly undone by how genuine, kind, and great you are. You're going to do immensely brilliant things and I can't wait to watch it happen. Thank you for being my friend.

Thank you to the friends I didn't name-drop. It doesn't make you less important or mean I don't love you. I just have memory issues, so let's laugh about it. You've all been supportive and loving (even before the surgeries when the darkness overshadowed me), and I'm keenly aware how lucky I am to have all of you in my life.

And most of all, thank you, dear reader. If you've been alongside me on this journey, from *The Absence of You* to now, I'm honoured. Regardless if you're a new reader or an older one, I'm honoured and humbled you've read my words.

I hope they've helped you, I hope they make you feel less alone, and I hope they inspire you to live fully. I hope you won't find a home in the sharp edges of some of these words, but if they bring you comfort and you do, please know that you aren't as alone as you feel.

Above all else, be kind to yourself, give yourself the grace to simply be, and put yourself first.

With gratitude,
Annie Sophie Le

WAYS TO CONNECT WITH ME

I am always undone whenever I hear from readers, from sharing your story with me, or even send me memes of cats. Thank you.

Email: annie@anniesophiele.com
Instagram: @anniesophiele

www.ingramcontent.com/pod-product-compliance
Lightning Source LLC
Chambersburg PA
CBHW020528080526
44583CB00013B/783